SUPER SEDIMENTARY ROCK

by Rex Ruby

Minneapolis, Minnesota

Credits
Cover and title page, © technotr/iStock; 4–5, © lucky-photographer/iStock; 6, © ValeryEgorov/iStock; 6–7, © Jithesh Sundar/Shutterstock; 7, © Douglas Rissing/iStock; 8, © Budanatr/iStock; 9, © LucynaKoch/iStock; 10, © Damocean/iStock; 11, © /Shutterstock; 12–13, © Christoph/Adobe Stock; 14, © kyletperry/iStock; 14–15, © Maxim Petrichuk/Shutterstock; 17, © elena_suvorova/Adobe Stock; 18, © William Daniell/Wikimedia Commons; 18–19, © Gonzalo Buzonni/Shutterstock; 20–21, © Imagesbybarbara/iStock; 22, © pornpimon Ainkaew/iStock, © New Africa/Shutterstock, and © AlenKadr/Shutterstock.

Bearport Publishing Company Product Development Team
President: Jen Jenson; Director of Product Development: Spencer Brinker; Managing Editor: Allison Juda; Associate Editor: Naomi Reich; Associate Editor: Tiana Tran; Art Director: Colin O'Dea; Designer: Kim Jones; Designer: Kayla Eggert; Product Development Assistant: Owen Hamlin

Library of Congress Cataloging-in-Publication Data is available at www.loc.gov or upon request from the publisher.

ISBN: 979-8-89232-032-0 (hardcover)
ISBN: 979-8-89232-509-7 (paperback)
ISBN: 979-8-89232-161-7 (ebook)

For more information, write to Bearport Publishing, 5357 Penn Avenue South, Minneapolis, MN 55419.

CONTENTS

A WAVE IN THE DESERT

There is a big wave running through the **desert** in Arizona. But it's not water. The Wave is a rock **formation** that took shape over more than 150 million years. The **slopes** on the Wave curve up and down. They have a pattern of reddish-brown and white stripes. How did this rocky place form?

The Wave formed during the time when dinosaurs lived on Earth!

The Wave

A ROCKY WAVE

The Wave is made of sandstone, which is a kind of **sedimentary** (*sed*-uh-MEN-tur-ee) rock. Sedimentary rock is one of the three main groups of Earth's rocks. The other two are **igneous** (IG-nee-uhs) and **metamorphic** (*met*-uh-MOR-fik) rock. All sedimentary rock forms from tiny pieces of rock called **sediment.**

Each of the three types of rock form in different ways.

Igneous rock

Sedimentary rock
Metamorphic rock

MAKING SEDIMENT

Where does sediment come from? It starts as bigger rocks. Then, water may break it up. As rain washes over large rocks, it slowly wears them away. Tiny pieces break off from the larger rocks. Over time, more and more of the big rocks wash away and become sediment.

Sand is a type of sediment. Each grain is made of rock.

Layers of sand

SEDIMENT ON THE MOVE

The same water may sweep the sediment along. Sometimes, sediment gets washed into a lake or a river. Eventually, the pieces settle on the bottom. Over the years, more sediment is washed into the lake. Layer by layer, sediment builds up at the bottom of the lake.

As wind or water carries sediment along, bigger pieces crash and break into smaller ones.

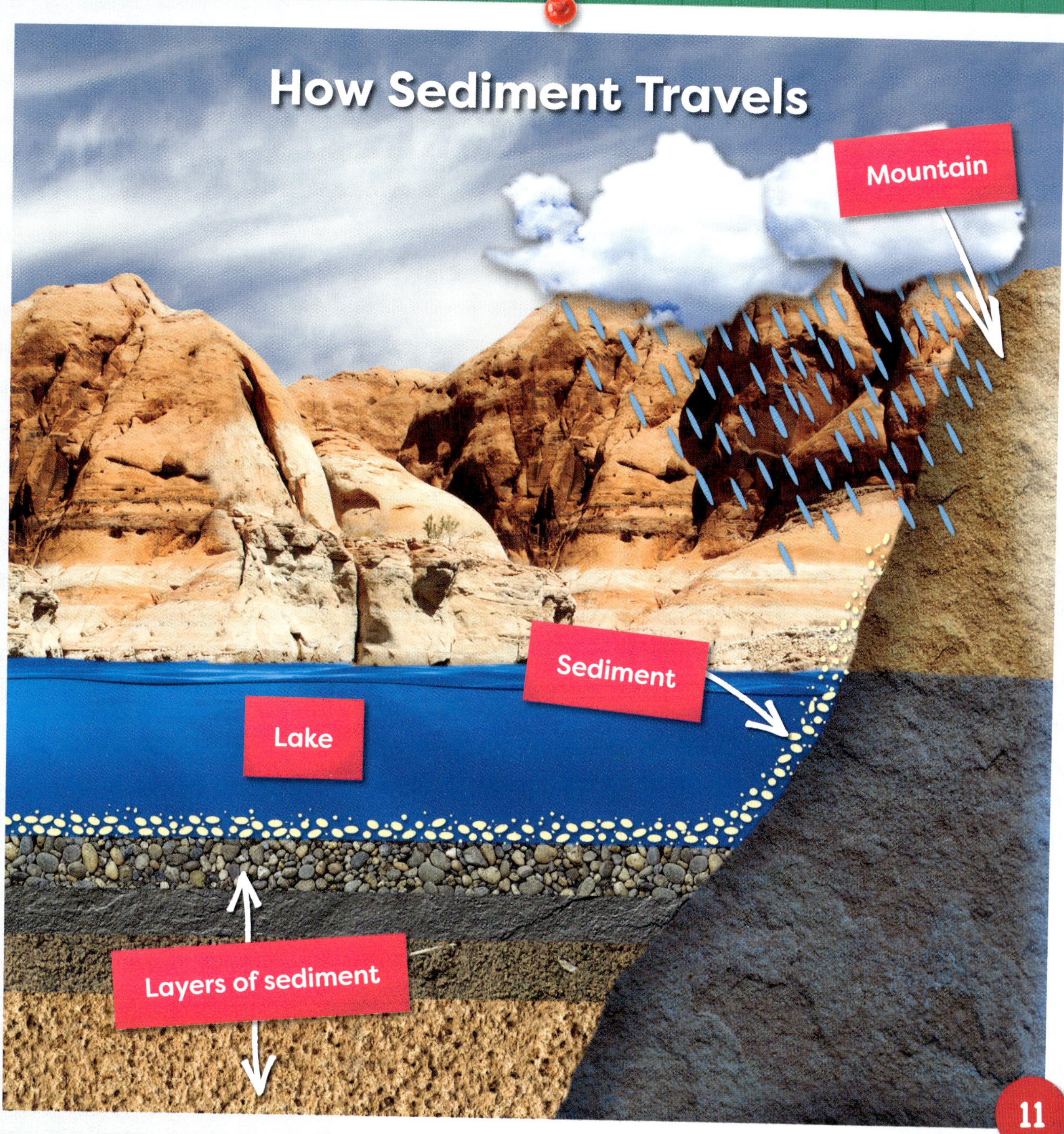
How Sediment Travels
Mountain
Sediment
Lake
Layers of sediment

TURNING INTO ROCK

As they gather, the layers of sediment press together. Over millions of years, they join to become solid new sedimentary rock. Each layer of sediment may have come from a different kind of rock. That is why sedimentary rock often has layers that are different colors.

The rocky pieces of sediment are made of **minerals**. That helps the pieces stick together.

The Rainbow Mountains of China are made from sedimentary sandstone.

MAKING ROCK WITH WIND

Wind can form sedimentary rock, too. Sometimes, the wind blows and picks up loose pieces of sand or dirt. When the flying pieces rub against large rocks, the rocks break off into smaller ones. Over time, this new sediment builds up on the ground. The layers eventually join together to make new sedimentary rock.

The Wave was formed from sediment made by the wind.

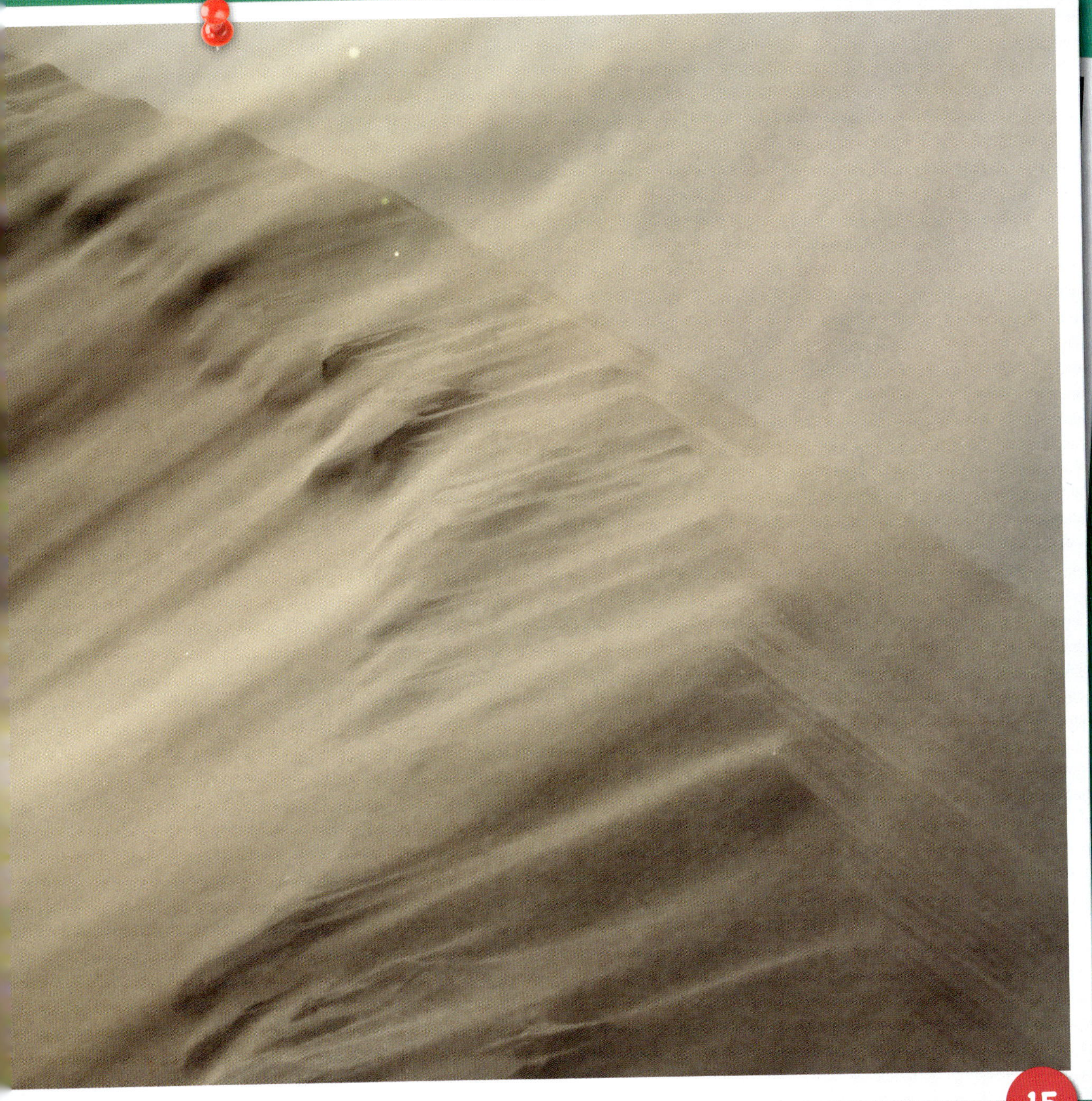

SHAPING THE WAVE

The Wave did not always have smooth, curved slopes. It actually took millions of years for the rock to get the shape it has today. That is because dusty winds helped carve the Wave's rippling, wavelike curves. As they swirled and swirled over the rock, the rock took the shape of the patterns in the wind.

Millions of years ago the Wave probably looked like a rough sandstone formation.

OLD MAN OF HOY

Another rock formation made of sedimentary rock is called Old Man of Hoy. This rock was once part of a sandstone cliff. Over many years, ocean waves crashed into the cliff and wore away the rock. This caused large chunks of the cliff to fall away. It left a rocky tower standing apart from the cliff behind it.

Old Man of Hoy used to look like a person standing on two legs, hence its name.

A painting that shows how Old Man of Hoy looked years ago.

Old Man of Hoy

ROCK HUNTING

Many people love to see all the amazing rocks on Earth. People called rockhounds collect cool rocks they find. There are many kinds of sedimentary rocks out there, and they each look different. That's what makes rock collecting so much fun!

Rockhounds find rocks in parks, mountains, beaches, and even deserts!

SCIENCE LAB

Make Sedimentary Rock in a Jar

Using real sediment, such as sand and pebbles, make a model that shows how sedimentary rock forms.

You will need:

- An empty glass jar with lid
- Sand
- A spoon
- Pebbles or gravel

1. Use a spoon to add some sand to the jar. Press it down with the spoon.

2. Add layers of pebbles and other forms of sediment, with each layer made of something different than the one before.

3. Keep adding layers. Make sure you press down on each one with the spoon.

4. When your jar is full, screw on the lid tightly.

GLOSSARY

desert an area of very dry land that is usually hot and covered with sand or rocks

formation a group of rocks or a large rock that stands out in an interesting way or has an unusual shape

igneous rock that forms from magma or lava that has cooled and become solid

metamorphic rock that forms when put under high heat or pressure

minerals solid substances found in nature that make up rocks

sediment tiny pieces of rock that have broken away from a larger rock

sedimentary rock that forms from layers of tiny pieces of rock

slopes lines or surfaces with one end higher than the other

INDEX

READ MORE

Burgan, Michael. *Rocks and Minerals (Weird But True Know-It-All).* Washington, D.C.: National Geographic Kids, 2022.

McDougal, Anna. *Sedimentary Rocks (Earth's Rocks in Review).* Buffalo, NY: Enslow Publishing, 2024.

LEARN MORE ONLINE

1. Go to **www.factsurfer.com** or scan the QR code below.
2. Enter "**Rockin Sedimentary**" into the search box.
3. Click on the cover of this book to see a list of websites.

ABOUT THE AUTHOR

Rex Ruby lives in Minnesota with his family. He likes going on long walks and discovering new rocks along the trail.